A Wag to the Wise

A Wag to the Wise

Lucie the Golden Retriever

Translated by

Joanna Howells
with
Oscar Fovarge

Red Hawk Books
London and Swansea

Red Hawk Books is an imprint of Red Hawk Media Ltd whose addresses can be found at

www.redhawkmedia.co.uk

Copyright © Joanna Howells and Oscar Fovarge 2021

Joanna Howells and Oscar Fovarge assert their moral rights to be identified as the authors of this work

2nd Edition

First published by Kestrel Books Ltd in 2010

A catalogue record for this book is available from the British Library

ISBN 978-1-9160843-2-2

Graphic design 2010: Eva Lissinger
Graphic design 2021: Adam Evans

All rights reserved. No part of this publication may be reproduced, stored in a retrieval system, or transmitted in any form or by any means, electronic, mechanical, photocopying, recording or otherwise, without the prior permission of the publisher and authors.

For Ray and Elizabeth

with love

from these wags to the wise

Contents

Introduction 9

Food 11

Human Relations 25

Survival Guide 43

Dogiquette – polite behaviour for the modern dog 57

Love 69

Creativity 77

Catology – understanding cats 87

Walkies 95

Dear Reader,

Welcome to my book of doggy wisdom!

In a fast-changing world, where the one- or two-dog household has replaced the togetherness of the pack, it is more important than ever to pass on as much wisdom as we can to our puppies. After all, we've reached a point where some believe that it's perfectly acceptable to share our servants and living spaces with cats! In short, it is our duty to prepare our pups for a radically different, post-pack society.

In the past, our youngsters learned from their mothers and pack leaders. But we are so well-off these days that our puppies move out of the puppy pen and straight into their own homes. This usually happens some time before they know the difference between a carpet and a lawn. It can place a terrible strain on the servants.

Let's be frank. It is important to recognize that our happiness depends on the wellbeing of our human helpers. Yes, we give them a great deal in return for their services. We offer them a structure to their lives and the unconditional affection they crave. They have become so much a part of our lives that they have even adopted many of our most famous proverbs and sayings. That is why I have included the human version of our wisdom – in a smaller font – as a guide to their thinking.

There will be dogs – stick-in-the-muds in my view – who will say that humans are backward and stubborn. True, they have never bothered to learn more than a few barkamatically wrong imitations of our language. They can also be whiny and sentimental. They are, by turns, rules-based yet hopelessly disobedient. They may well be lazy, eat too much and take too little exercise. Many also take years to domesticate to our needs, at the same time being too eager to please (an infuriating combination, I have to admit). Worst of all, you might think, is their failure to develop a full coat of fur, for convenience, if nothing else. (Seriously, how did that happen?)

Yet, when growl comes to bark, they are, on the whole, a remarkably loyal and hardworking breed. If we are the woof of the world, they are the weft. As the great Saint Bernard once thought, "If we bite them, do they not bleed?" We are big enough to give their wisdom, however wrong-headed or copycat in some cases, a place alongside (or slightly below) ours.

Lucie - the Golden Retriever

Food

More haste, less feed.

More haste, less speed.

One swallow doesn't down a fishbone.

One swallow doesn't make a summer.

Beggars can be oozers.

Beggars can't be choosers.

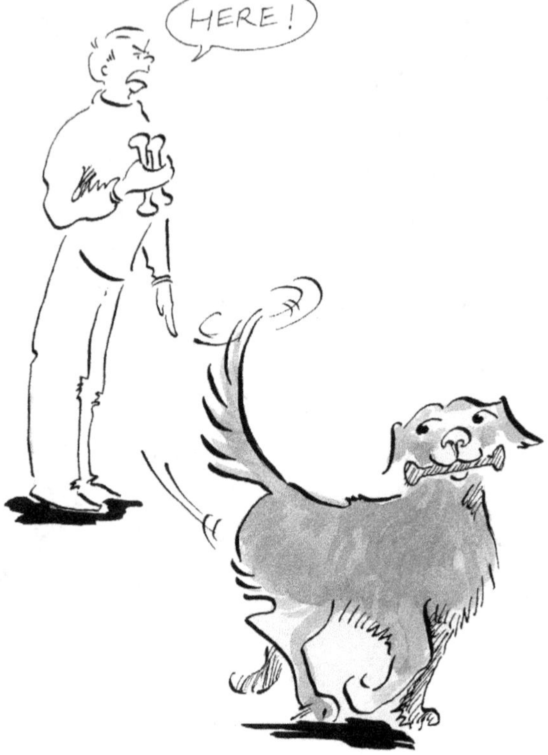
HERE!

A bone in the mush is worth two in the hand.

A bird in the hand is worth two in the bush.

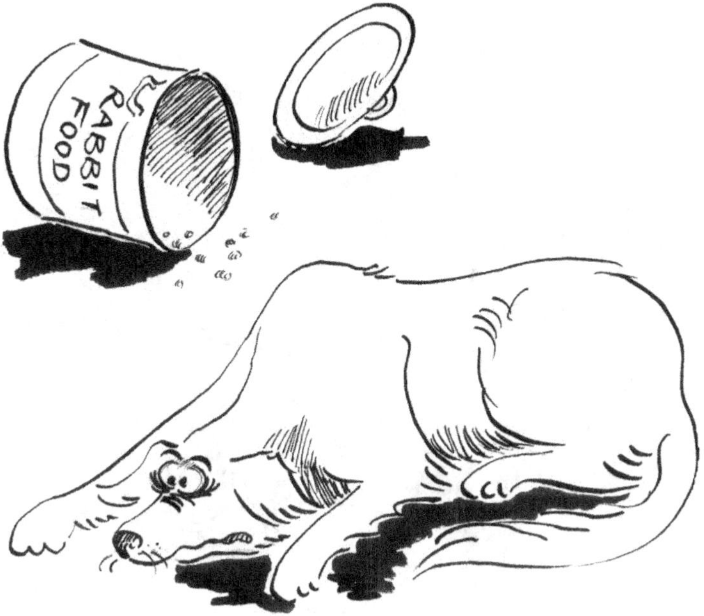
RABBIT
FOOD

It's easy to be sick after the event.

It's easy to be wise after the event.

Outside every thin dog is a fat one trying to get in.

Inside every fat person is a thin one trying to get out.

Forbidden suet is the sweetest.

Forbidden fruit is the sweetest.

A friend in greed is a friend indeed.

A friend in need is a friend indeed.

Half a sausage is better than none.

Half a loaf is better than none.

I can have your cake and eat it.

You can't have your cake and eat it.

When one store closes another store opens.

When one door closes another door opens.

Human Relations

If at first you don't succeed cry, cry and cry again.

If at first you don't succeed try, try and try again.

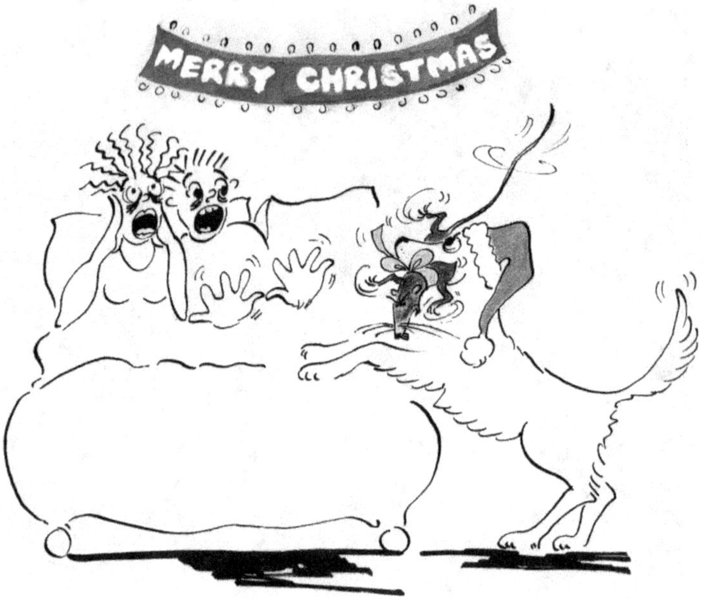
MERRY CHRISTMAS

It's the thought that counts.

Ditto

Fools rush in where mongrels fear to tread.

Fools rush in where angels fear to tread.

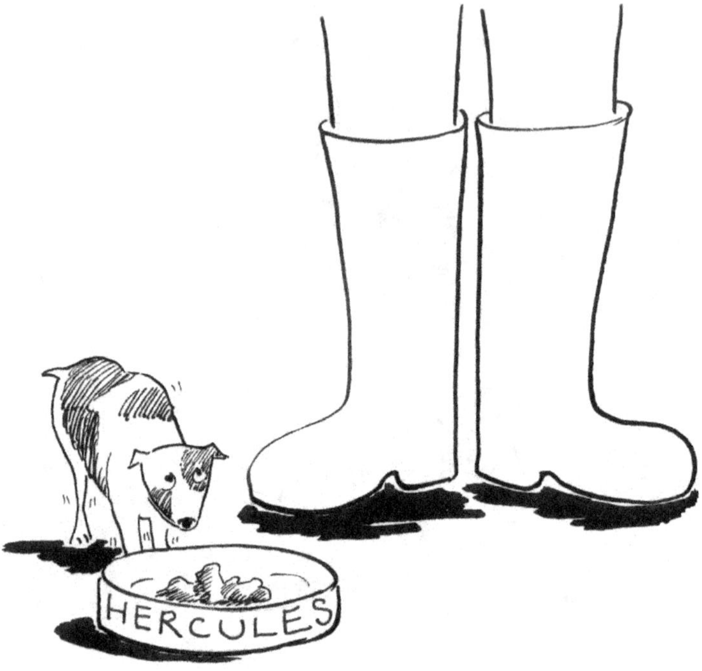
HERCULES

Give a dog a bad name and regret it.

Give a dog a bad name and hang him.

It's an ill wind if nobody feels any better.

It's an ill wind that blows nobody any good.

Postmen flee a hundred times before breakfast

Cowards die a hundred times before their deaths.

Never underestimate the lick of the Irish.

Never underestimate the luck of the Irish.

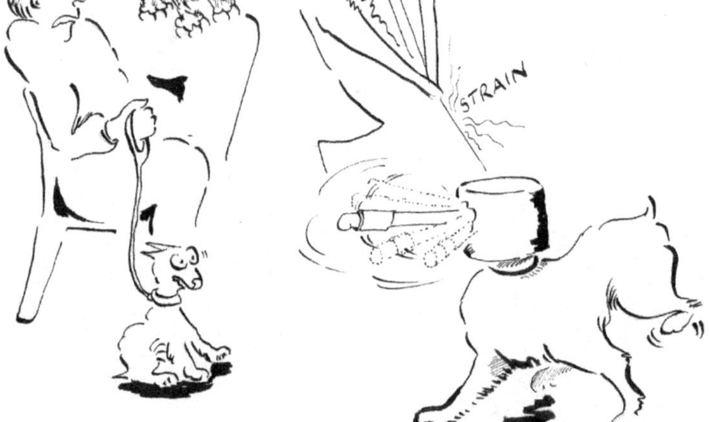
RECEPTION
STRAIN

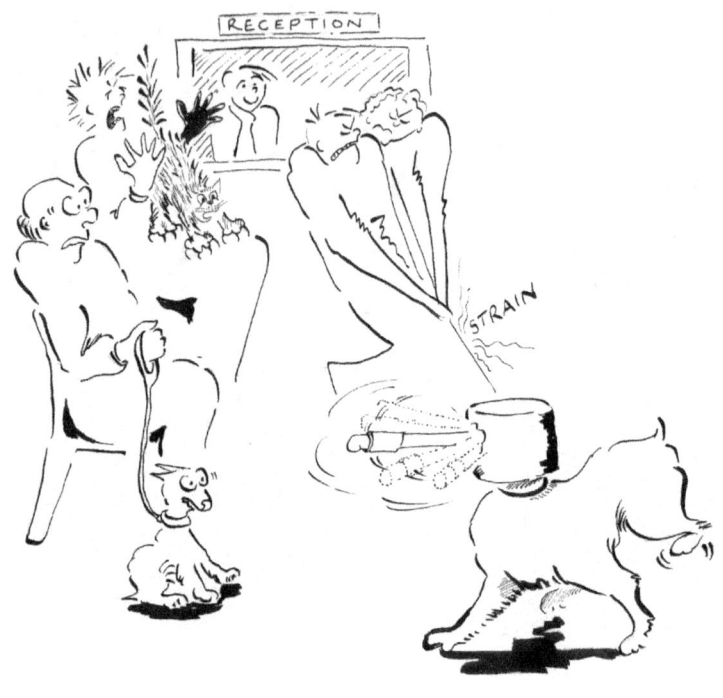

Where there's a vet...

...there's a bill.

Where there's a will there's a way.

All work and no play makes Jack a dull Russell.

All work and no play makes Jack a dull boy.

The early dog catches the postman.

The early bird catches the worm.

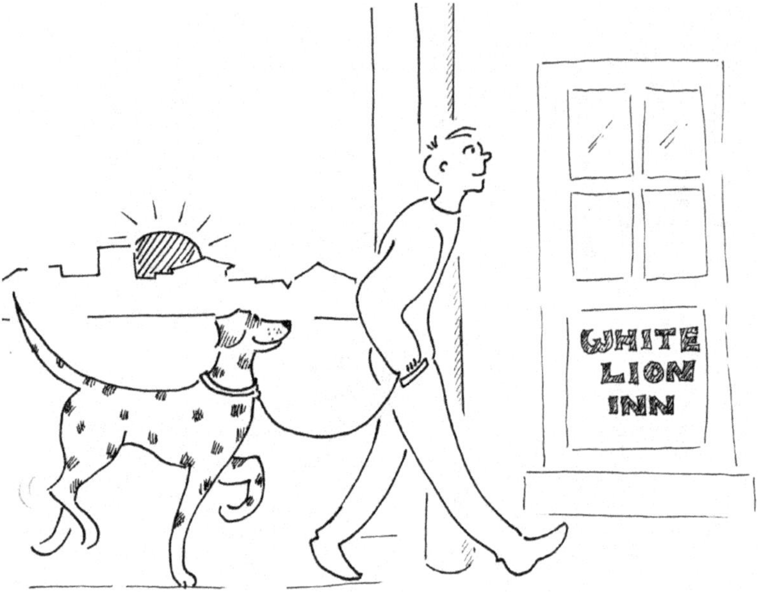
WHITE
LION
INN

A dalmatian doesn't...

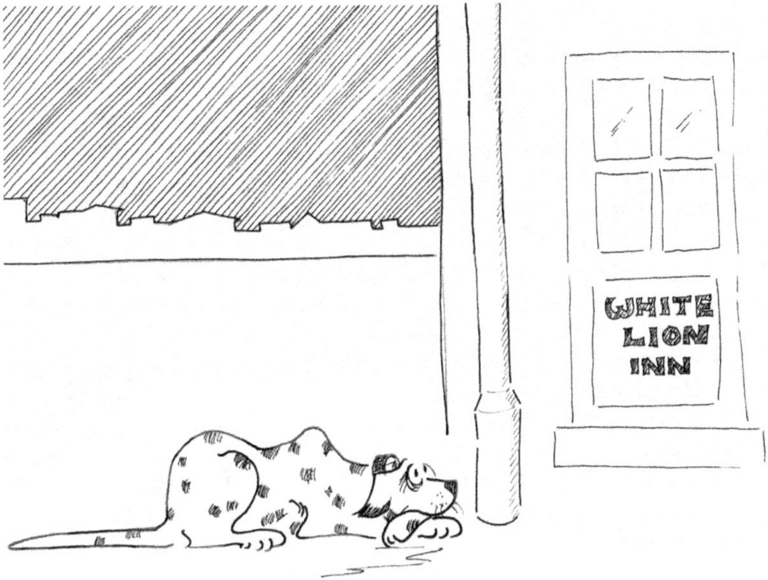
WHITE
LION
INN

...change its spots...

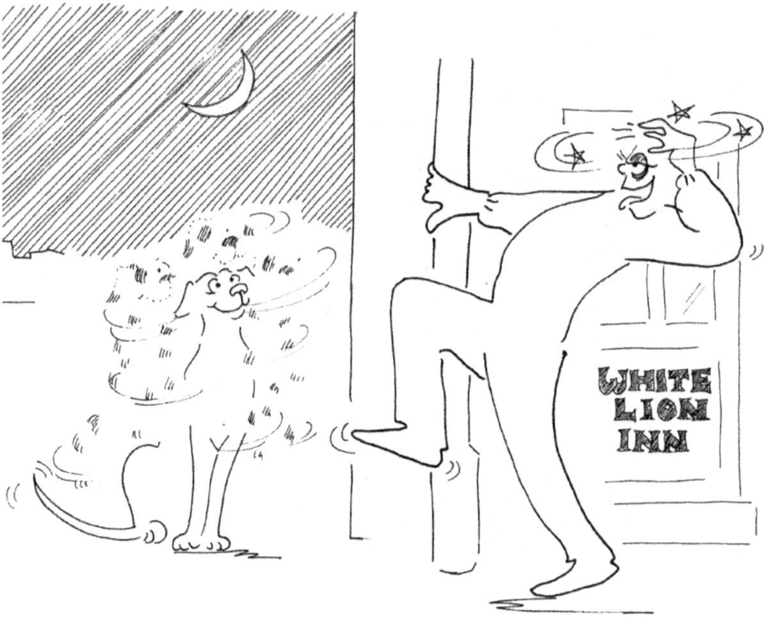
WHITE
LION
INN

...or does it?

A leopard doesn't change its spots.

I've got a shoe and I'm prepared to lose it.

I've got a gun and I'm prepared to use it.

Survival Guide

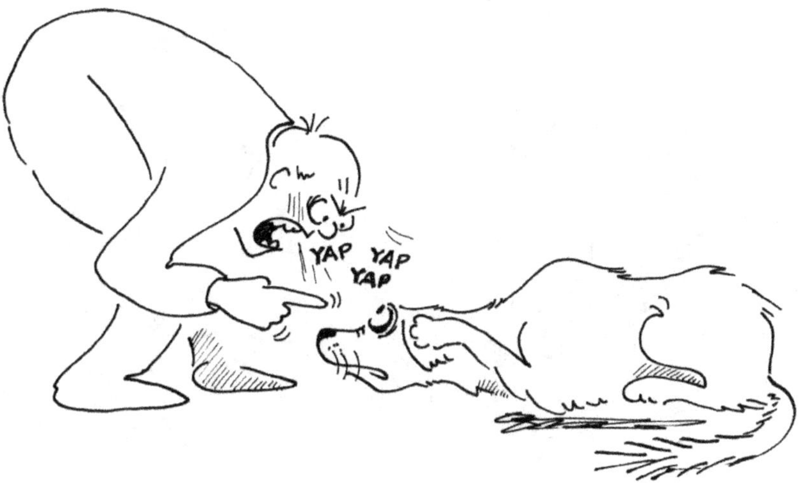
YAP
YAP
YAP

Barking servants seldom bite.

Barking dogs seldom bite.

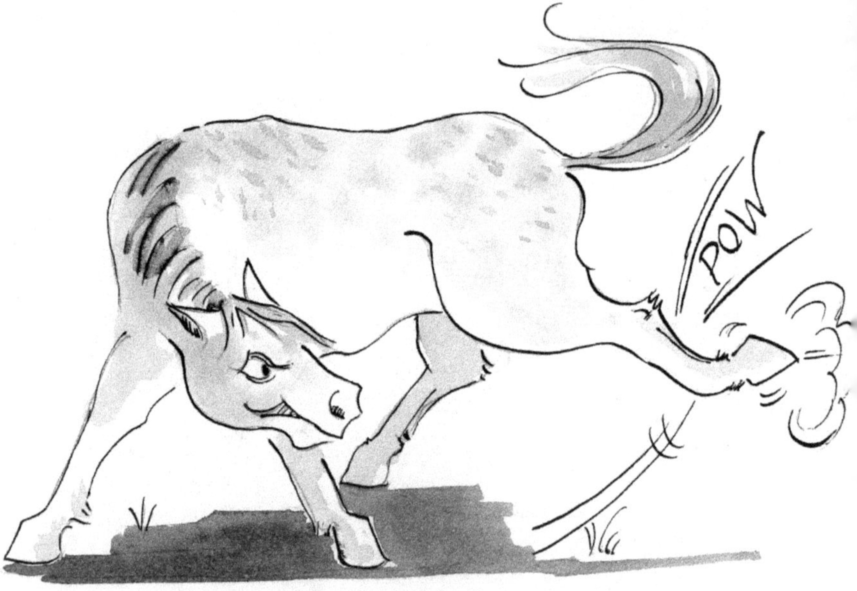
POW

Never approach any given horse from the south.

Never look a gift horse in the mouth.

Out of sight...

....

....

...out of mind.

Ditto

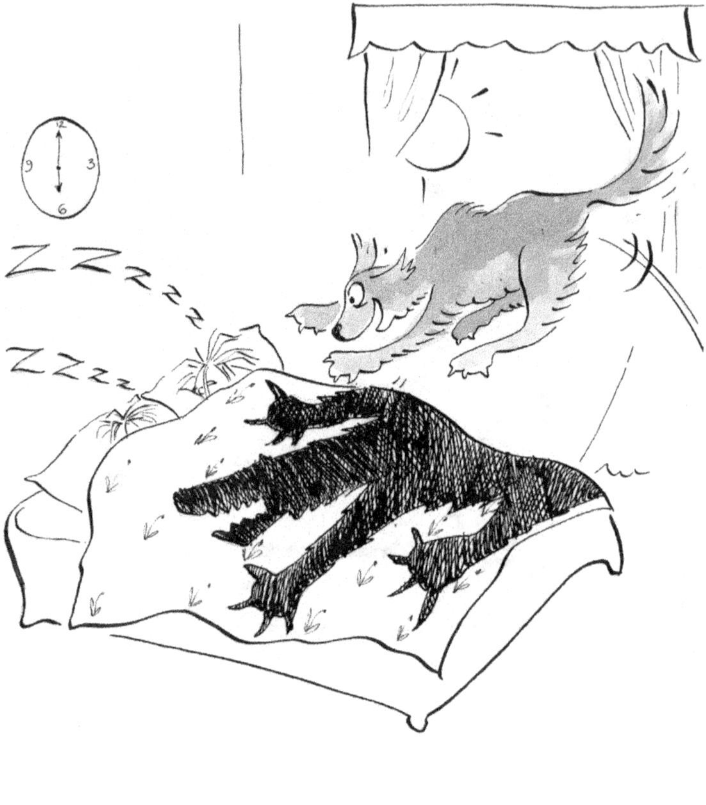

ZZZzzzz
ZZZzz

Let sleeping servants lie.

Let sleeping dogs lie.

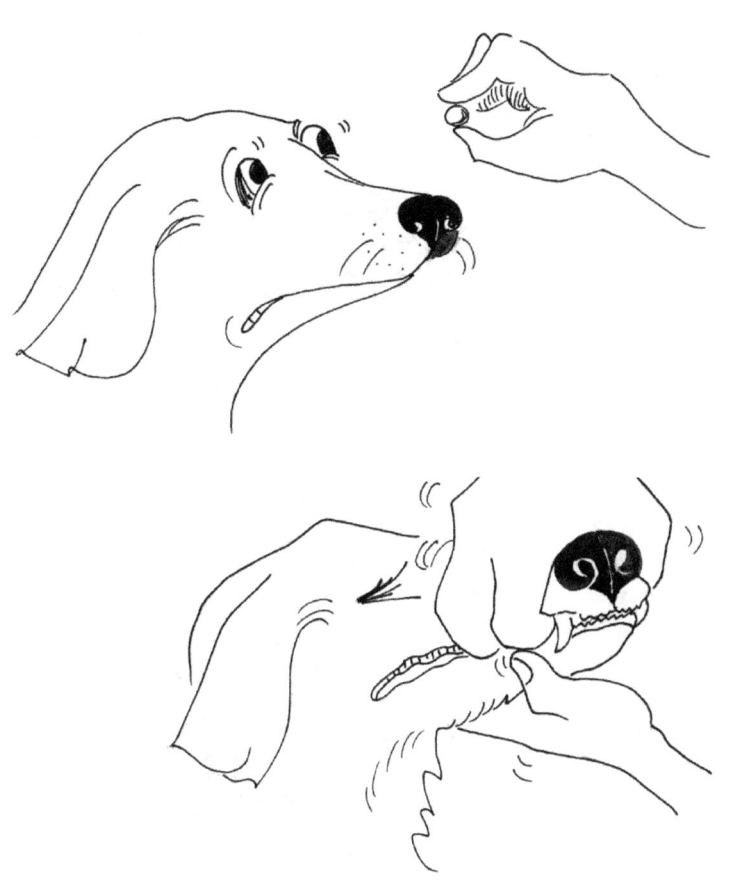

Where there's a pill...

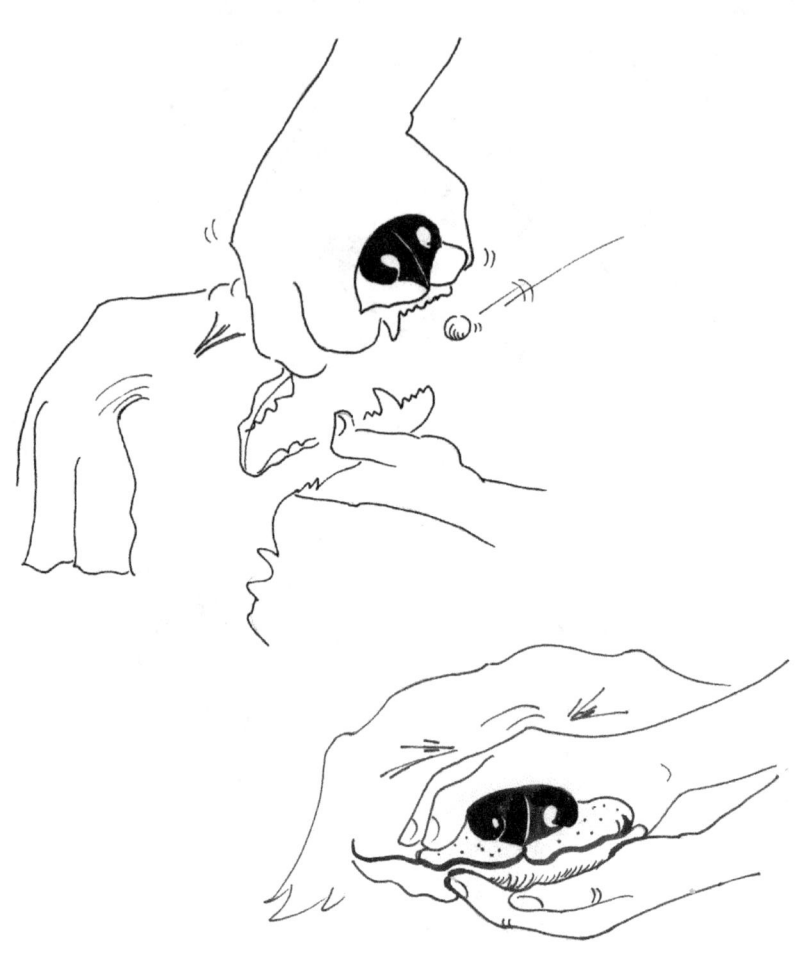

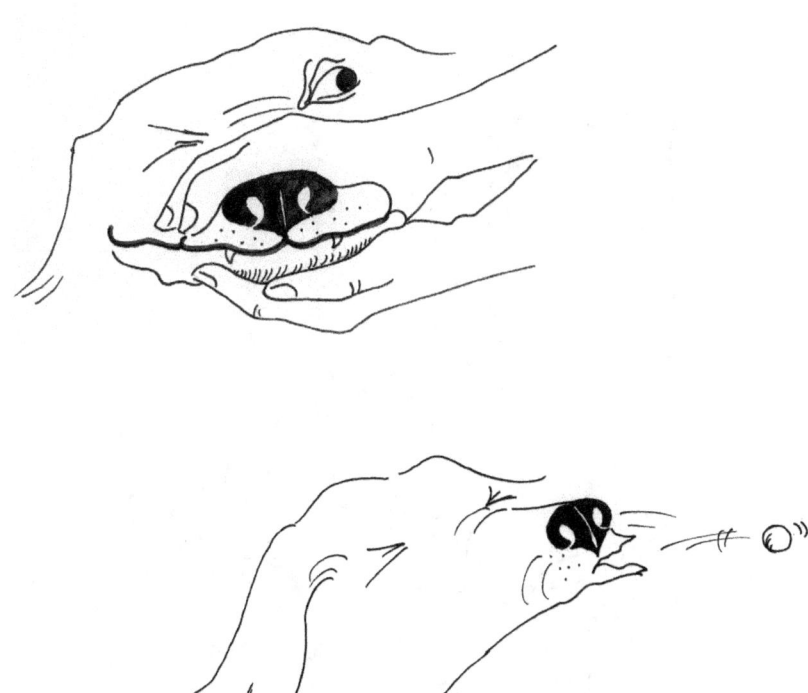

... there's no way.

Where there's a will there's a way.

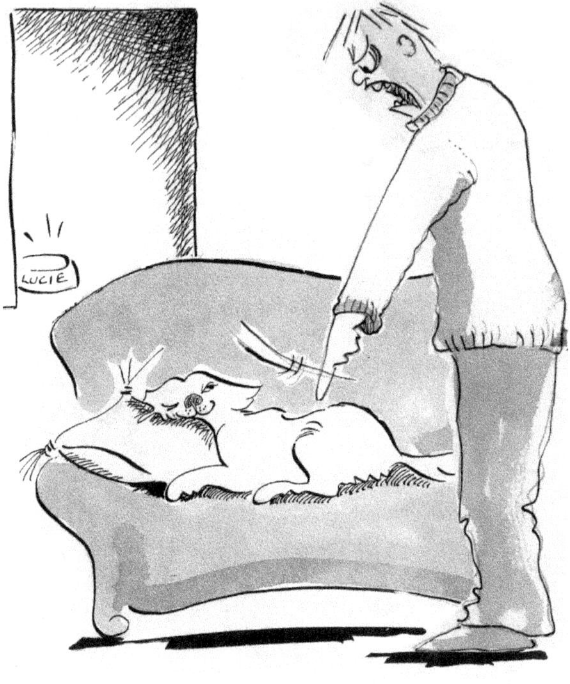
LUCIE

Don't cross your servant before you've been fed.

Don't cross your bridges before you come to them.

Dogiquette

The proof of the poodle is in the greeting.

The proof of the pudding is in the eating.

Don't keep all your pugs in one basket.

Don't keep all your eggs in one basket.

Do keep all your pups in one basket.

Don't keep all your eggs in one basket.

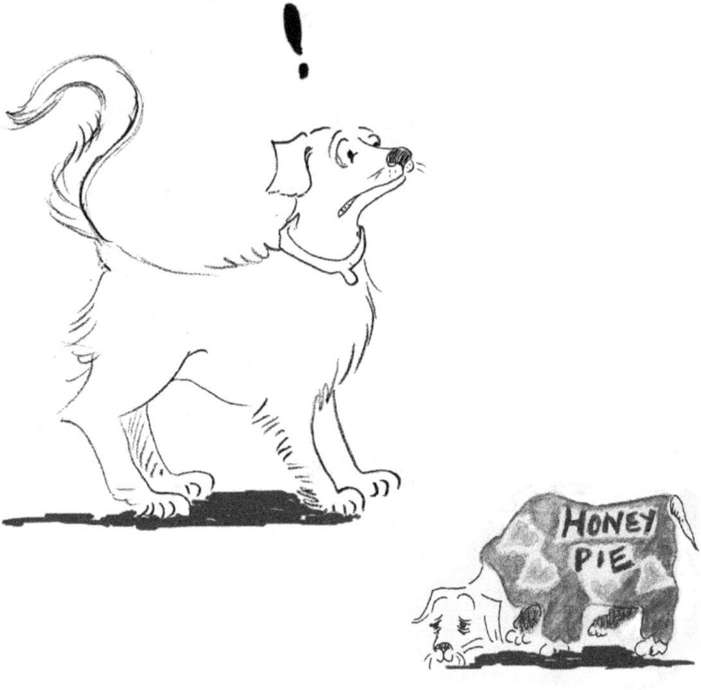
!
HONEY
PIE

Help a dog over a lame style.

Help a lame dog over a stile.

You scratch your back and I'll scratch mine.

You scratch my back and I'll scratch yours.

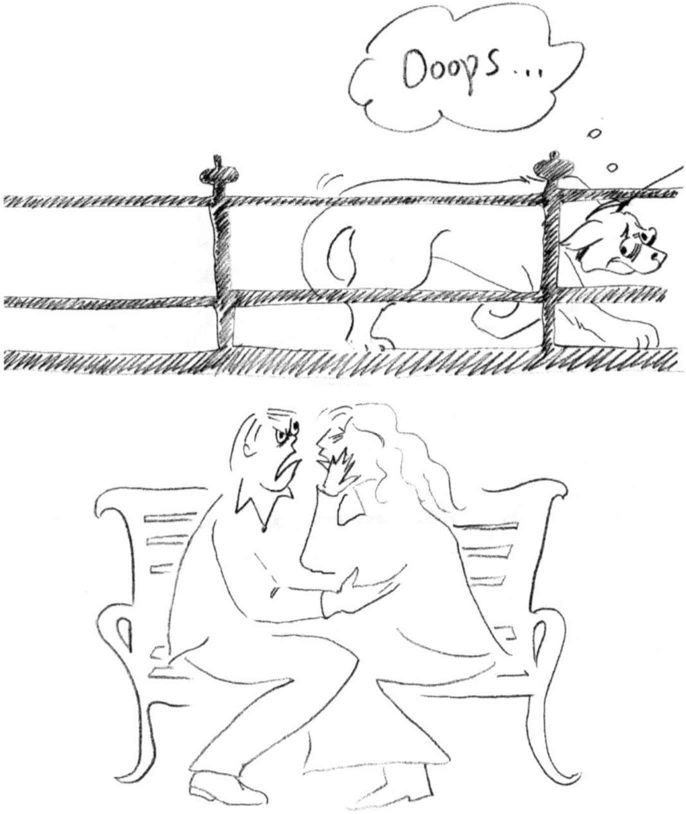
Ooops...

Look before you leak.

Look before you leap.

Piddle your own canoe.

Paddle your own canoe.

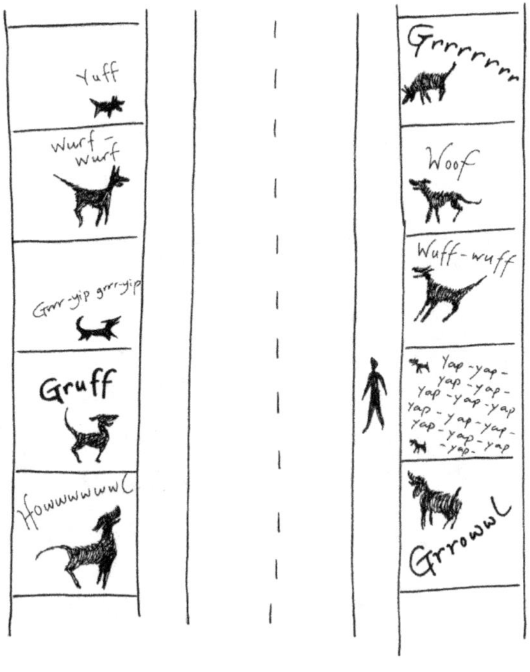
Yuff
Wurf - wurf
Grrr-yip grrr-yip
Gruff
Howwwwwwwl
Grrrrrrrr
Woof
Wuff-wuff
Yap-yap-yap-yap-Yap-yap-yap Yap-yap-yap-Yap-yap-yap-yap-yap
Grrowwl

Every dog has its say.

Every dog has its day.

Love

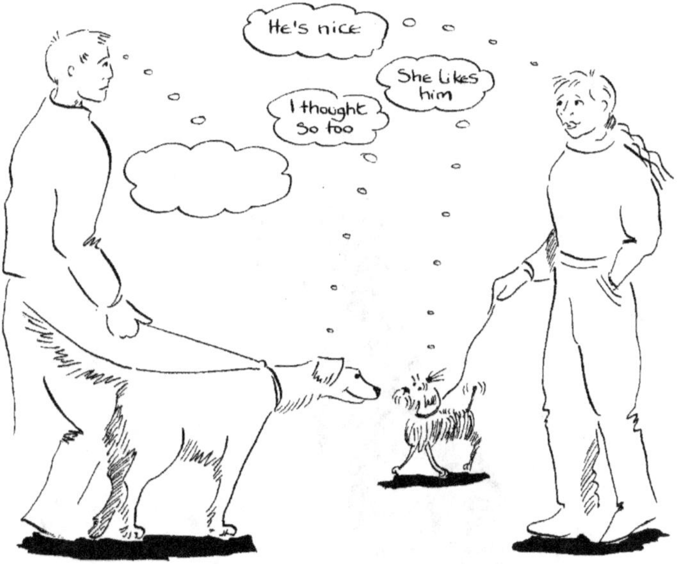
He's nice
She likes him
I thought so too

You can lead a man to water, but you can't make him think.

You can lead a horse to water, but you can't make it drink.

A bitch in time...

...makes nine.

A stitch in time saves nine.

Six of one and half a dozen of the other.

Ditto.

Don't go barking up the wrong she.

Don't go barking up the wrong tree.

Creativity

If a hole's worth digging it's worth digging well.

If a thing's worth doing it's worth doing well.

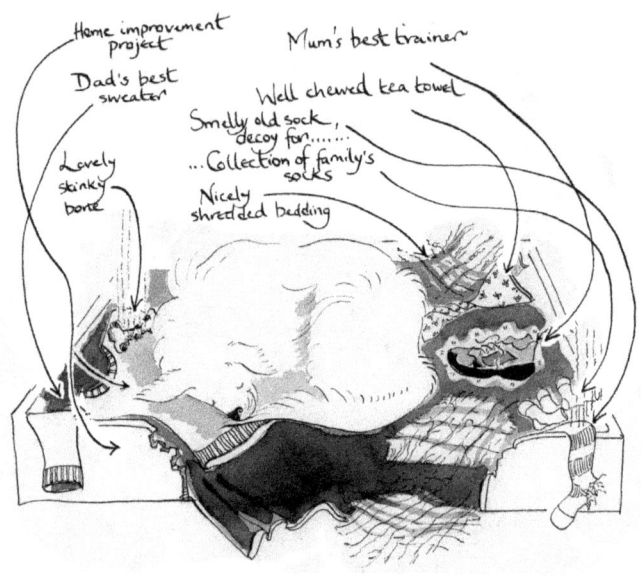

Home improvement project
Mum's best trainer
Dad's best sweater
Well chewed tea towel
Smelly old sock, decoy for......
...Collection of family's socks
Lovely stinky bone
Nicely shredded bedding

As you make your bed so you can lie in it.

As you make your bed so you must lie in it.

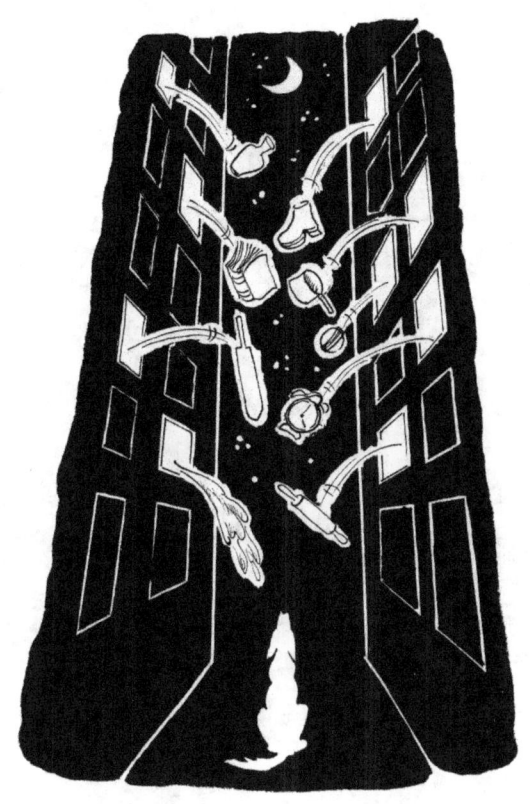

All things come to he who wails.

All things come to he who waits.

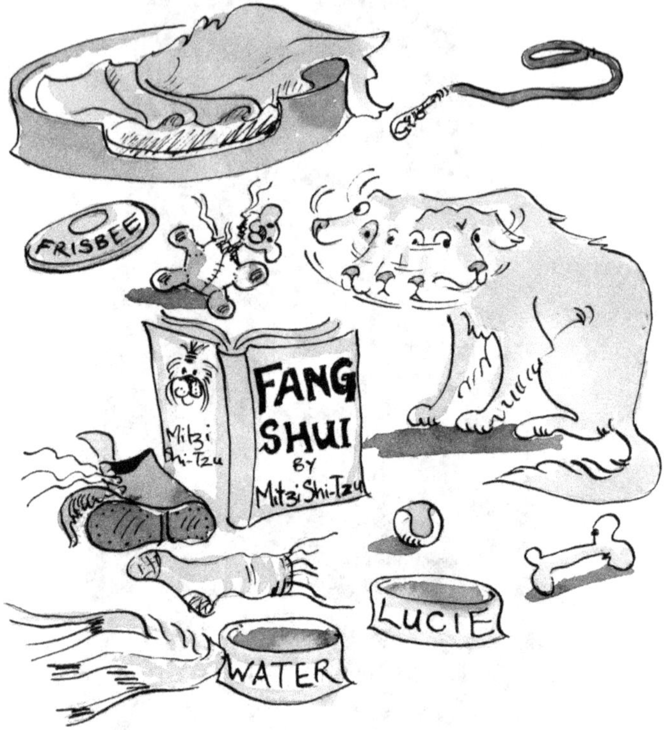

FRISBEE
FANG SHUI BY Mitzi Shi-Tzu
Mitzi Shi-Tzu
LUCIE
WATER

A place for everything and everything in its place.

Ditto

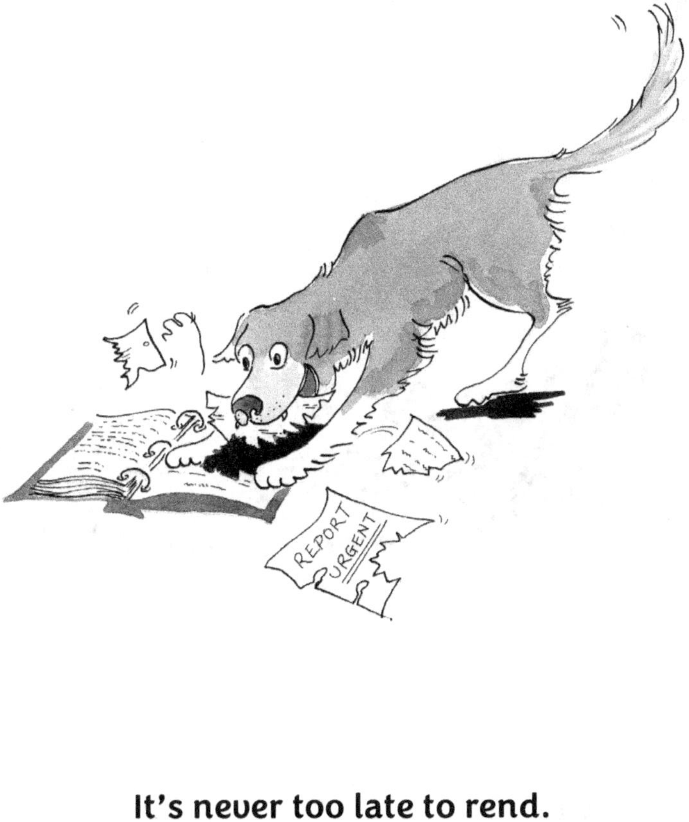
REPORT
URGENT

It's never too late to rend.

It's never too late to mend.

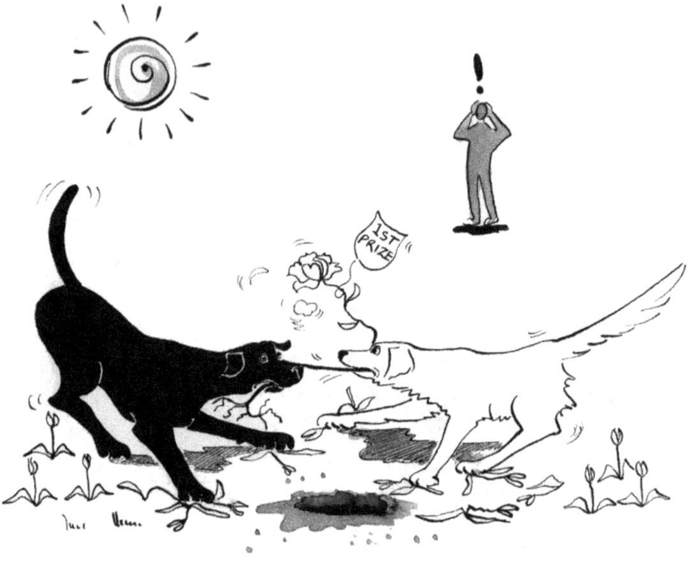
1ST PRIZE

Lay waste while the sun shines.

Make haste while the sun shines.

There's no smoke without ire.

There's no smoke without fire.

A rolling dog gathers moss.

A rolling stone gathers no moss.

Catology

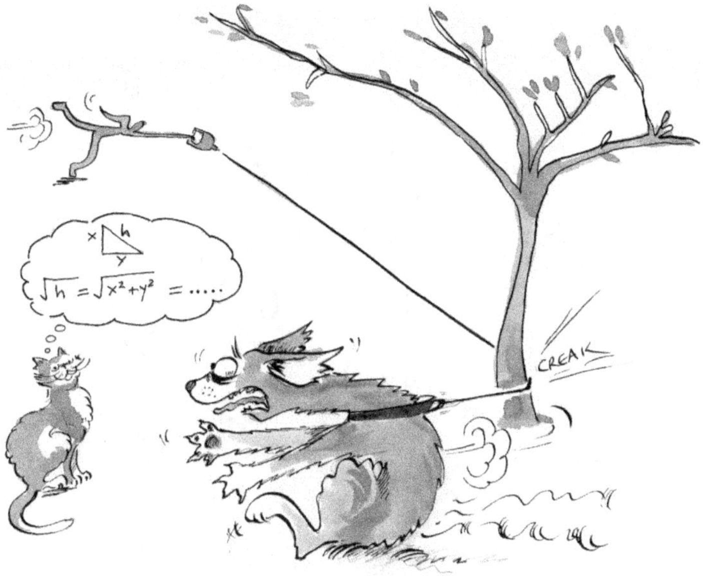
x
h
y
$\sqrt{h} = \sqrt{x^2+y^2} = ...$
CREAK

It’s a long lead that has no ending.

It’s a long road that has no ending.

You can't teach an old mog new tricks.

You can't teach an old dog new tricks.

When the servant's away the cat's at bay.

When the cat's away the mice will play.

There's more than one way to scare a cat.

There's more than one way to skin a cat.

Walkies

Cross the puddle where it's deepest.

Cross the stream where it's shallowest.

All that retrieves

....

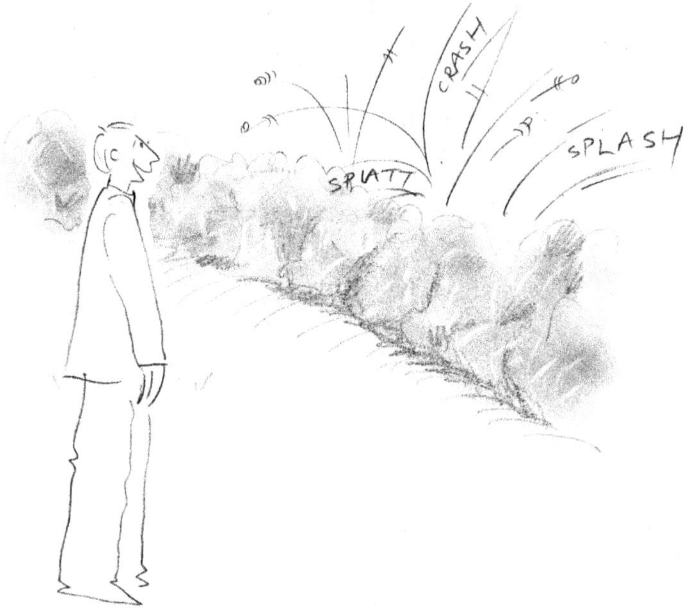
SPLATT
CRASH
SPLASH

•••••••••••

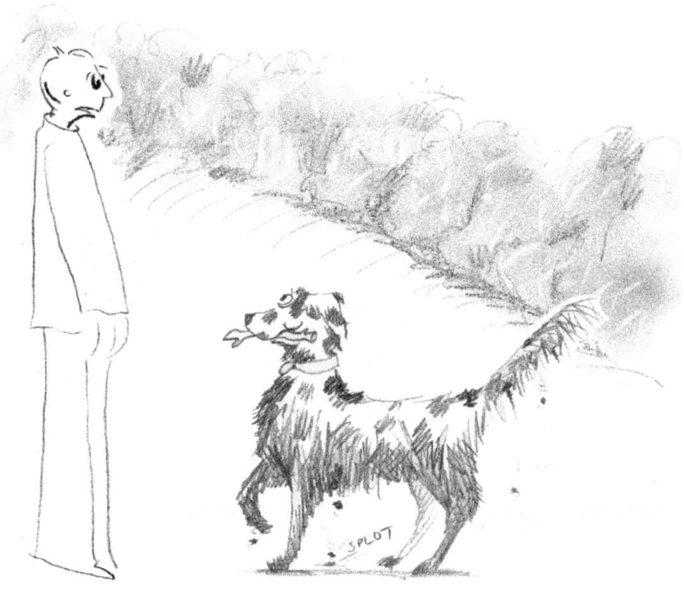
SPLOT

is not golden.

All that glitters is not gold.

Mud...

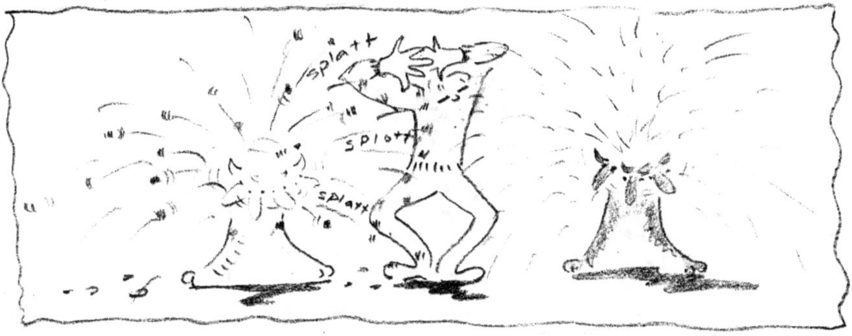
splatt
splott
splatt

...is...

...thicker than water.

Blood is thicker than water.

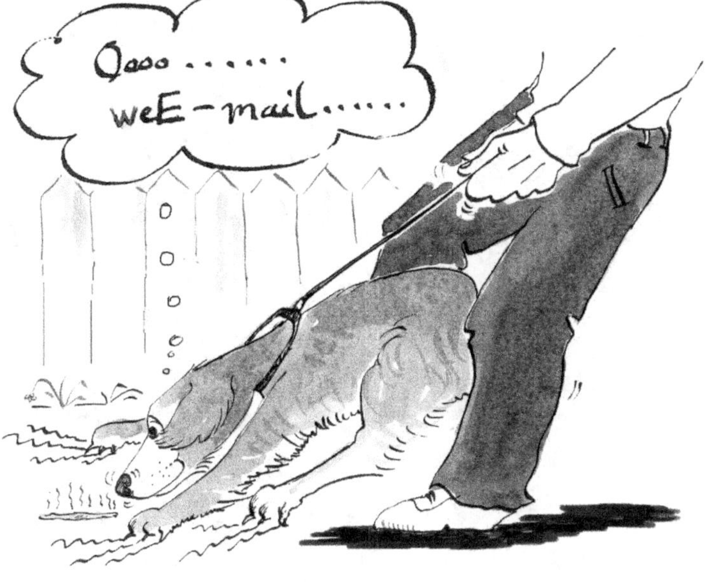
Oooo ......
weE-mail......

The road to the newsagent's is paved with good in-scent-ions.

The road to hell is paved with good intentions.

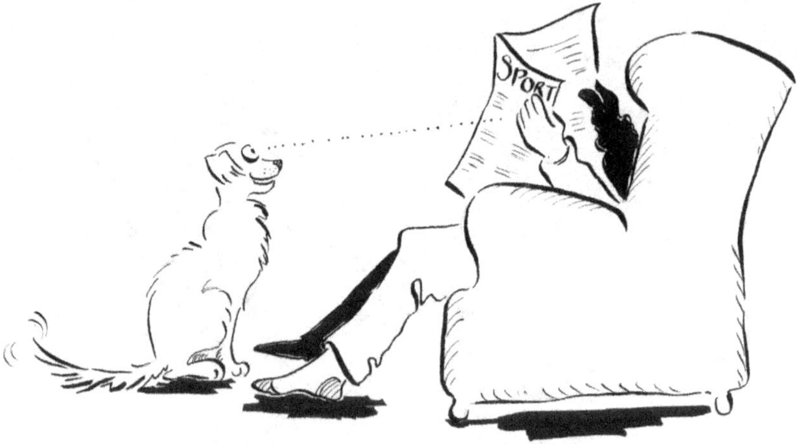
SPORT

A watched servant never walks.

A watched pot never boils.

Having...

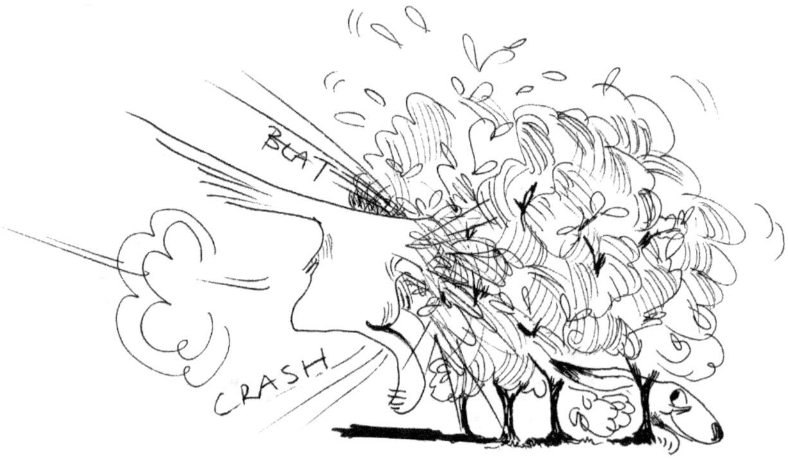
BLAT
CRASH

....

a bad hare day.

Having a bad hair day.

Well, I'll be dog gone.

Well, I'll be doggone.

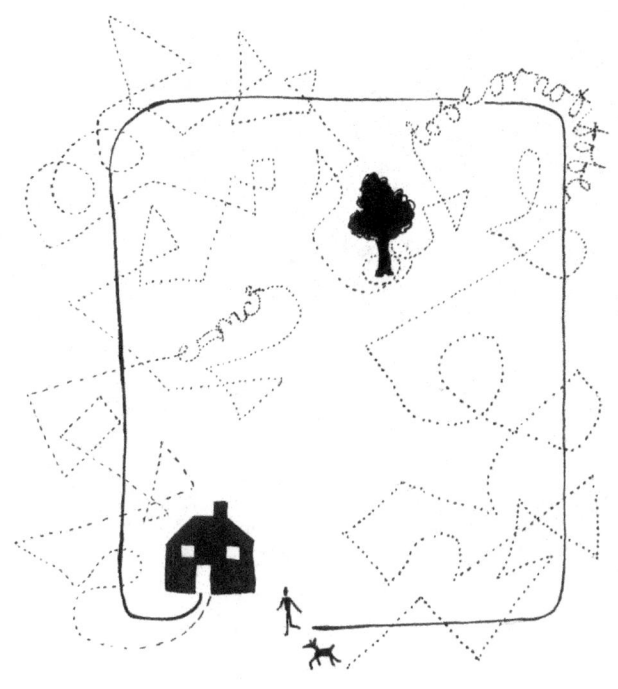

All roads lead to home.

All roads lead to Rome.

www.ingramcontent.com/pod-product-compliance
Lightning Source LLC
Chambersburg PA
CBHW071528080526
44588CB00011B/1589